Understar

Understanding Heaven

Stephen Guppy

Wolsak and Wynn · Toronto

Typeset in Garamond.
Printed in Canada by The Coach House Printing Company, Toronto.
Front cover art: "Oracle" by Nelly Kazenbroot
Cover design: The Coach House Printing Company, Toronto
Author's photograph: Nelly Kazenbroot

The publisher gratefully acknowledges
the Canada Council for the Arts
and the Ontario Arts Council
for their generous support.

The Canada Council | Le Conseil des Arts
for the Arts | du Canada

ONTARIO ARTS COUNCIL
CONSEIL DES ARTS DE L'ONTARIO

Poems included in this book have been published in the following journals: *Ambit,
Grain, Quarry, Stand, The University of Hawai'i Review,* and *Whetstone.* "Language Arts"
won second prize in the Scottish International Open Poetry Competition;
"Ultrasound" was a finalist in the Lexicon Poetry Contest.

Wolsak and Wynn Publishers Ltd
192 Spadina Avenue, Suite 315
Toronto, Ontario
Canada M5T 2C2

National Library of Canada Cataloguing in Publication Data
Guppy, Stephen, 1951-
        Understanding heaven

Poems.
ISBN 0-919897-79-7
I. Title
PS8563.U577U64 2001   C811'.54   C2001-902391-X
PR9199.3.G86U64 2001

for Nelly, Sebastian, and Isabel,
and for my mother and father

CONTENTS

PART ONE

MY MOTHER IS CRYING

She is standing at the kitchen sink,
framed in a perfect square of sky,
drying spoons and melmac breakfast bowls
with a polka-dotted dish towel
and sobbing so her thin back heaves,
as if something about the summer light
(the drifting cirrus clouds, perhaps,
the rippling leaves, the swallows)
has filled her with a grief too huge
for the cells of her heart to encompass.

I am part of all this too, of course: I am
five years old; I am walking very carefully,
placing my feet on the faint black lines
between the sky-blue lino tiles. I am balancing
on a net of wires, beneath which
there is nothing: the sky
without sunlight or scimitar
moon; the Devil, who stinks
of rust and blood; the rusty
hinge of my mother's crying. I know
in my bones this is my fault, of course.

Whatever upsets her
is part of my body, a weight
beneath my skinny ribs,
a devil-box that makes me dance
precariously over the blue,
breathless heavens, balanced
on the wires of her crying. *Step
on a crack, break your mother's back.*

My mother is crying.
Her hands grip the towel.
Her heart is a window, a doorway,
through which I take one giant step,
and fall with my hair streaming upward
like smoke from a stunt-plane,
an acrobat teetering
out of his skin, plunge
endlessly into the angelic light
on the slick kitchen lino, the warped violins
of her sobs bound and knotted
like snares on the bones
of my clenched, helpless hands.

UNDERSTANDING HEAVEN

isn't easy, which is why, I guess,
we're out here, the whole family
gathered on the lawn
after nightfall, staring out
of the small, separate
caves of our selves
into starlight. My father
looks through binoculars
at the quivering lights of Orion
scanning the sky
for the one blood-red cell
of the orbiting Gemini capsule.

We kids hang back by the chipped
concrete porch, wishing we
could leave or smoke, go back
in the livingroom, maybe watch some TV.
"That's it!" our old man finally shouts,
pointing vaguely toward
the Big Dipper, where,
undeniably, a nondescript
corpuscle, red as a spark,
is methodically describing
its arc on intractable darkness.

"That's only an airplane!" my sister
complains, and I mutter
along with her, though secretly I wonder
at the man within that grain of light,
who alone knows what it is to be
adrift beyond the map of days,
whirling through the horoscope
in tensile equilibrium
between the fragile lights of waning earth

and the terror of falling, just falling
infinitely out of his childhood,
diving up from the inverted sky
into nothingness, the spaces between
the integers he prints in his scribbler
(little boy with his blonde, corny brush-cut
sitting rapt in a hot Midwest schoolhouse),
the letters and words of his name.

I stare at the lawn, feigning boredom.
My father, smiling, hands me the glasses.
"Maybe someday," he says,
"you kids will go there," meaning space,
and then repeats it
like a spell against the mundane lives
he must know that we'll
fall into, the failure of
his dreams for us, his own
becalmed ambitions. He must recognize,
as well, that this night is the last
and only time we'll stand like this,
four tributary strangers,

who, having given up,
voluntarily, the right to be
innocent, earthbound, enfolded in
the family's pale, exalted light, have chosen
to allow ourselves to drift apart,
carried off by the dense gravitation
of sex and money, grief and work,
our many insignificant,
unforgivable betrayals. When the speck

of fading red has passed
beyond the daylight
rim of earth, and arcs
obscurely over other lives, we gather
the shards of our fragmented
selves, and enter
again a house which holds between
four simple walls all magnitudes
of hope, and loss, and distance.

1. '52 Austin A40 (One owner–low mileage)

My father is standing in front of his car.
His legs, in baggy Air Force pants,
obscure its skinny Dunlop tire. One hand
rests on my sister's neck; the other
cups my shoulder. Like Jesus, he is staring
above us into vacant air; his arms
are open, outstretched
in apparent supplication: he is saying,
Take these children—This boy, this girl.

In heaven, which, like everything else,
is monochrome, non-committal,
our washed-up gods prepare themselves
for the sacrifice he offers. My sister's eyes
begin to glow; her hair lights up, a web of sparks.
My own eyes burn like opals. The miracle begins

to whirl us up, though like everything
divine, it takes a lifetime. In other
pictures, other parts of our lives,
we will give up our vague, indeterminate souls
atom by shivering atom: for now,

we squirm and roll our eyes
fidget in our polished shoes,
unaware that our parents have set us adrift,
and grin into Mother's black camera.

2. '32 Chevrolet (custom)

I never saw it, but was often told
how my father cut the body
of his touring car in half
to make a pick-up, removed
both doors for ease of unloading
spare parts and his mechanic's tools
from the space behind the bench seat. This
was the car he drove to meet
my mother at the steamship docks
in Vancouver when she came here
on a train of British war-brides
that had carried her five thousand miles
depositing at intervals
a woman at each whistlestop
and cluster of shacks on the prairies.
I imagine how she must have felt
inching gingerly down from the unlikely height
of the platform toward her future life
knowing no one but the soldier who,
his uniform traded for a scratchy black suit,
grinned impatiently out
of his weird homemade truck
to welcome his new wife
to nowhere. Her mind, I imagine,
was still filled with light—
the light of the Atlantic swells,
animate and spiritual; the coarse brittle light
of Saskatchewan snow; the frail lights
of train stations mired in the night
where girls as young and lost as she
were dumped like sacks of unread mail,
the women who remained
on the train looking back,

some sobbing, some clutching
their newborns. My mother,
the last of the brides on the train
stepping down from the door of the Skyliner Car
in her best rose-print frock
and her Rita Hayworth heels
and feeling as if she is falling
through the watercolour sky of Vancouver, B.C.
and into the lumpy, stained passenger's seat
of her husband's mechanical centaur. All the way
home to his rooming-house, she has nothing to say:
the world, like the car, seems divided;
behind her is England, the Old World, the past,
while up ahead there is only rain,
a landscape of smears and erasures,
the sheer cliff of vertigo
that plummets from her breastbone,
some pine trees, a sloped road, the sea.
The hybrid car rattles and farts into the future.
My father witters confidently on
in a voice that is English and isn't,
and my mother smiles bravely
through her lipstick and rouge,
half her soul wafted like bleak west-coast rain
toward this inescapable snare she has made
while the other half telescopes endlessly back
to the vanishing point of her childhood.

3. '57 Plymouth Savoy (mechanic's special)

It's seven o'clock and I'm headed for school.
I put on my wool toque and scratchy cloth coat
and wave to my father as he pushes the car
away down the driveway and over the hill
to his job as an auto mechanic. I watch
as he vanishes, gathering speed
and wait for the cough as the engine fires up
and my old man jumps into his Plymouth.

Every morning it's the same routine.
When the car starts, it's miraculous,
the universe uttered from a virtual point,
dragon's teeth budding forth armies;
when it doesn't, I catch up to him,
lean my skinny arm against
the finned ass of the Plymouth,
and listen to my father curse
the dead weight of the life he's made,
a man who has wounded his hands on machines
who gives up his breath every day of his life
breathing flickering life into
the recalcitrance of matter.

"Nothing works," he says, and grins to make up for
the fatigue in his voice. I grin too
and push at the Plymouth,
ready enough to take my place
beneath the futile weight of things,
though unable to, being no one
yet, a kid in his parka and home-knitted toque
who can only smile back at his father's
unease, reflecting stark light like a mirror.

The two of us grunt, and the wreck begins to roll.
"Nothing works," my dad reiterates, and smiles again,
making a joke of the one truth he's managed
to refine from the dense, gravid atoms
of memory, history, circumstance, fate;
trying hopelessly to shield his son, as fathers always
fail to do, from the fatal light of manhood.

Nothing works, he says. *Nothing works. Nothing.*

4. '59 Vauxhall Victor (lady driven)

You can make it, she says, and I'm wondering
whether she means I can make
it through the intersection in
this gutless English car of my mine
that used to belong to my older sister
before somebody hits us or
that I can pull over anywhere,
take her back to the dank basement suite
I share with a somnambulant roommate
or just drive to some power-cut or dark, unused driveway
and peel off her Levi's and the trashy black bra
she boosted from the sale bin at Woolworth's.

You can make it, she whispers, the wounded ellipse
of her mouth at my shoulder, her hand
sliding over my heart like raincloud
eclipsing the everyday light of my senses
and revealing, simultaneously,
a future of side-swipes and head-on collisions,
a freeway grid of fatal choice, dead-
man's curves through which we drift,
exhilarated, gasping for traction.

The moment, like everything else
important in life, ends badly—the car bucking futilely
back into traffic, and the girl laughing,
half in scorn, half in something
that may be relief, and it won't be
until a couple of weeks later that we'll finally have
each other, the two of us struggling
to yank up our jeans at the sound of her mother
clattering up the staircase in push-over heels, but always
what remains in my mind is that moment
of forked understanding, that heartbeat

of coupled meaning lodged between
our two excited heartbeats. 30 years
from that blink of elided binary code
to the fractals of branching interpretations
that open from each keystroke, I can visualize
her perched on the bench seat
beside me, ikonic as the Sybil,

a pouting Catholic logger's daughter
with her tight mohair sweater and black leather boots,
the bruises from her father's fists
on her breasts and thighs and shoulders,
and a voice that says *Yes, You can make it.*

SLEEPING OUT

Each year, in faltering summer, we move
out of our parents' lives, into the bare, browning spaces
of all the identical lawns in the suburb, each yard

flowing endlessly back
through the past toward forests
so dense that they emanate

silence and darkness, the whole of the night
as it seeps through our tents. We watch
from the border of light as our parents

repeat familiar rituals, passing
from room to room, fastening
screen doors and shutting off lights.

The windows flash their semaphore
from house to house; then finally
our rows of neat yards bleed into fields—

primordial, devoid of light,
pure night below the arc of stars,
under which, with the mindless grace of beasts,

we sprawl across our sleeping-bags
and breathe the smell of canvas. In their beds,
our parents lie like stones, their dreams

a dark topography
through which our whistling voices speak
like wind at an open window. When the last

of the bedroom lights
dulls out, and the frayed whip
of stars burns its weal down our backbones,

we rise out of childhood, our cocks
and budding breasts alert, and folding back
the canvas like a caul, a spent

cocoon, go out,
aimless through the barren streets
of heaven, so transparent

in our stone-washed jeans
and t-shirts dyed the colour of sky
the blue cones of the streetlights pass

clear through us, and the river
of hours we wade through
leaves no watermark on our skin.

Our sneakers utter nothing
as we pad between the sidewalks
wordless, feral, freed of the weight

of our parents' irremediable desires, we recover
the primitive desire to walk the earth
in darkness, neither hunters

nor the prey the hunter's
mind creates, but merely
what is left when the diurnal self

goes liquid; boils clear; reveals
the simple animal need
to be, to breathe

in moon-white air the ozone scent
of our own youth, honed by midnight
to a knife edge. Unafraid, we prowl the sleeping lawns

of our neighbours, wanting nothing
but to lean against their doors like the ghosts
of unremembered passions; to listen

for their gentle, unreflective breath; to hear them
turning like silt in their mineral beds—
adult bodies warm as soil,

though ossified, made rigid
by the weight the needing heart creates, the terrible
gravity of loving. Toward dawn, when the first

of our fathers has risen from sleep
and is already groping his way
through the unlit rooms

of habit, we return to our sleeping selves,
breathing in bell-tents. Curled up
in our duck-down bags, with only

a flag of unruly hair breaking the chrysalis,
we wait as the world
rediscovers its borders, maps out

stark perimeters
of fence and drive
and dew-wet lawn, our bodies already

becoming stone, hard ore in alluvial rivers.

CRUISERS

You've probably seen them often enough
around town: men in softball team jackets
or worn leather coats, shoulders
hunched, their faces
flexing like catchers' mitts
awaiting pop fouls, worrying
at some private and utterly
commonplace grief. You've noticed them
out of the corner of your busy life, guys
in their thirties, or in late middle age,
coming out of the 7-11 in
no hurry at all, getting into the muscle cars
they might as well drive, having no more use
for mini-vans or sensible wagons.

You know, if you've been around at all,
where the orbit of their damaged lives
leads them: every night they go back
to the house where they once lived,
to the woman who is someone else's
wife now, or no one's; to the kids who resemble
the script of her scorn more than anything
human, especially
that bastard who used to be
their father. Every night
after midnight, when the streets are deserted,
they appear beneath the windows
of their lost children's bedrooms, the Camaro
in Low and the headlights dug under,
and sit staring up, through the haze
of cigarette smoke, imagining
not the imprint of their vanished selves
on the buttery light of the bedroom,
the ghost of a man with his child in his arms

making whole again the remnants
of his mortgaged hope, the shard
and seed and twisted pod, but rather
the taunting mirror-image
of the man who'll take his place.

And if you've known them, perhaps
looking down from your own bedroom window
at your own father's beating heart, diminished
to shuttered parking lights, the blue plumes
of car exhaust and distant
cigarette smoke, or perhaps
if you have been that man and know
how it is to have slipped, to have fallen
inside yourself, into the drag
of your own gravitation,
then perhaps you have already decided
that what motivates them isn't
psychology, but physics—the curvature
of time and space, bent inwards by the force
of loss, so that everything they know and own
is projected inexorably backwards
toward a singularity, the one true
point of origin, the moment when
they opened fists
they'd closed in grief or anger,
and saw the future turn to ash
and ribbon through their hands.

I open the shade, and clouds flood uphill,
morning fog the length of the valley
obscuring the farmhouse and fences and barns
that lie below our burned-off lawn
and the nondescript streets of the suburb.

Too wide-awake for bed, I take
my jeans from the bedpost, moving carefully
and quietly as I can to the door
so's not to wake my wife and son,
and tip-toe across the silvered planks
of the screened porch, into memory. The snails
have left their shining tracks
on the concrete of the garden walk; a few crows
throb from tree to tree, and the pheasant
who lives beneath the blackberry vines
on the rail fence struts and nickers. Below me
the dairy farm is all one cloud—the grey,
begetting light of dreams
flows slowly up the valley.

I pick my way around the mud,
the cow-pies stuck with flies and straw,
angling down the sidehill
toward the unseen farmhouse,
walking in and out of patchy fog
like a man who is lost in a forest
progressing from clearing to clearing
without ever locating
a fenceline or road. Halfway
downhill between the fence
and whatever lies below, I pause
and see myself reflected,

transfixed on the green, glaucous surface
of the murky pond next to the farmyard,
against the glare and skirl of mist,
cloud-fire, the green flames of jack-pines.

I bend to touch my shadow's hand
reaching up from the inverted sky,
the brother I loved but could not save,
the twin whom I left to go under and drown
in the fathomless pool
of his incomplete soul,
whom I mourn now, as the dead mourn
their bodies. I remember
his names, and recite them as I fall
one slow, careful step at a time down the hill
toward the rusted, steel-roofed barn
and the shape of the farmhouse below me

in which, forty years ago, I could easily
have been born, and farther
and farther away from my past
and my wife and my child, still asleep
in their warm beds of ossified
time, far above

this vague hour I travel through, waking.

PART TWO

My daughter, who is 20 months,
is lying on the livingroom floor,
plucking words from her brother's story-book
as if they were Cheerios
or berries from the garden plot
and eating them like candies.

Each time she believes
she's caught a word, she places the tips
of her stubby fingers up to her mouth,
makes a sucking noise, just as if she were pulping
the memory of each luscious sound
she's ever heard or dreamed of,
and giggles as she reaches for
the next word of the fable.

Curious, I lie down on the carpet
next to my little girl and, reaching
past her busy hands,
pretend to take a couple of words
from the illustrated story. She giggles again
and grins at me as I pluck my words
like windfalls from the virtual shade
of the fairy-tale forest
and touch them to my lips. She's right: they're good;

they taste like night, like the smiles
of wolves; you can hold them in your mouth,
cup them on your tongue like stones
worn smooth by the pads of snow bears.

They taste like salt, like the skin of your hand
when you lick it after hours of work
weaving straws of gold from golden straw
in the blunt crayon sunlight of August.

They taste like the ice
in the Wicked Queen's heart,
so cold that your bones burn like x-rays
and your teeth are the strokes of the wood-chopper's axe
in the bodies of half-transformed foxes.

"Daddy eat!" my little daughter says, and I do
just what she tells me: pick
the bitter, inky fruit from trees
and spiky bushes bright as blood;
crush them on my tongue and taste
the winter hush before my birth,
the chrysalis, the blind brown seed,

primeval forest shade between
the winding paths of stories.

ULTRASOUND

My wife lies on the metal bed, her cairn-
round body stripped and greased. The nurse
probes with a sensor. Myopic, incapable
of seeing past my nose, I peer
through moirés of faltering
light for your shape, leaning in
toward the life to come, our linked
unwritten future. *See the eyes?*
the prim technician asks,
and yes, the twin black half-born buds
take cautious shape, protruding
from their orbits. Then hands,
the fingers linked by webs, the nut
of the frail skull, your spine
curved like a sine wave. My little
amphibian, you swim
toward me from some flawless source
of light, which still contains you.
Where you are is on the page before
the story of your life, which is unfolding
word by implausible word from the dark
of this phosphor screen
trembling with jittery light
where you hover in created space
neither archetype nor being.

Twelve hours from the first
geological convulsion, you summon up
a final gasp and thrust your hips
toward the surging waves of pain—
our boy's scalp bubbles slowly out
of the bloody, hurt cleft of your labia
his flaming hair a remnant of
the fields of burning grass through which
his molten soul has travelled,
deafened by the cries of birds
shrieking with his mother's voice.

He opens his occluded eyes; his fluid sight
solidifies, an instant transmutation
from mercury to bounded mass, dimensions
of light and cold inventing themselves
in one lurch out of uterine darkness, the hole
in the heart sucking shut, the twisted
umbilicus grey as a cyclone. The doctor
deftly clamps the cord
lifeless now and taut as wire
and cuts our boy adrift from God;
from the eyeless enfolding Leviathan
of your cramping womb, formless
as the world before language;
from the answering pulse
of your heartbeat. When the midwife
has done with her rote examination,
thumping his frail pigeon chest
with her finger-tips, stroking
vernix from his tender folds, clearing
the veiled eyes of verdigris,
rotating the hips in their ball-joints,

I pick him up and listen to
his ragged, experimental
breathing. Open
the petals of his perfect hands.
Touch his palm and feel the fist
close firmly on my finger. Hold him
to my ear like a nautilus shell
and hear the lunar pulse of tides
through which he swam forever, safe
through each of the elemental ages

and out of which, twenty years from now,
he will slowly and finally sound.

CHANGING

Awakened for the second time
tonight, I stumble out of bed,
disoriented, groggy
as a drunk, and take my child
from his mother's side,
his mouth still seashell pink
and wet from the breast,
his perfect fingers
flexing like anemones. After laying him down

on the changing table, I open
the venetian blind on budding dawn
and blink into the sunrise. My son
wakes up without a sound; his body
fills with milky light
as if he is inhaling
the promise of distant solar heat,
all the ripe summer hours

of his childhood. My clumsy fingers
wrestle with the straps
of his soggy, clinging diapers; I force
my drifting brain to concentrate,
dab Vaseline on the folds of his crotch,
fasten the velcro tabs, scratchy
as cats' tongues, and heft him as gently
as I can to my shoulder. Outside,

the world has turned to gold;
the rooftops glow with stolen flame. Oblivious, snuffling,
more asleep than awake,
my boy lets his golden head
loll to my shoulder

and turns his face,
his needful, sucking mouth
and lapis eyes toward me,

willing, though unprepared,
like any son

to face the annihilating
fire of a father's love.

THE TEAR

Six weeks from giving birth, you bend
away from the lip of the bath
where I lie—bodiless, wholly immersed
in our lives—to show me
the wound where our newborn son's
head split your skin
as he shuddered his way
into being. The stitches
have vanished, but a thin ridge remains
a doubting mouth pursed
on the secret of your pain,
still fading like a bone-bruise
into memory. I touch your thigh
and think of stone—of fissures
in the quaking heart, fault-lines breaking
earth from earth, the luminous
veins in marble. What you love most
has torn you, dross from ore, refined
from who you might have been
some shattered but more perfect self,
strongest at the mended rents
as welded iron is strongest.

I lie back in the lukewarm bath,
let water rise above my ears,
struck stone deaf in amniotic churning,
watch you as you turn from me,
and wonder what it is to be
torn, to have forced yourself over
and over again into grief, the blade
of relentless love rending your skin,
dividing your life from the dream of your life,
forcing you over and over
the rift between being and bodying forth,
your faultless heart torn and triumphant.

DRINKING BREAST MILK

The taste is a nondescript
sweetness; the tongue,
cupped like a rain spout
beneath the pink thumb
of the nipple, curls up
in astonishment, expecting, if anything,

mere blandness, the chalk taste
of milk, and receiving, inexplicably,
the white scent of a winter moon;
rainy daylight filled with the calls of birds;
the last hours of autumn dissolving.

What surprises, though, is plenitude;
how generous the body is, leaking pools
on the sheets where you lie,
staining the top of your housecoat. At night I wake,
my arm soaked with milk, nuzzle closer
to your sleeping breasts, extending
my tongue like an anteater: blind, burrowing

Pleistocene mammal, the whole
of my body an undulating throat
that spasms unbearable sweetness—

rain out of thunderheads, rivering down
to the desert and arroyo,
the dry, bitter fields

the parched earth,
the prophesied harvest.

BUILDING A DOLLHOUSE

—for Isabel

1. preparations

I lay out the implements I'll need for the project:
Claw-hammer; tiny brads; screwdriver; glue;
a handful of silver screws, whorled like the shells
of obscure fossil mollusks from underground seas;
spirit-level; tape-measure; carpenter's square;
the smell of my own childhood bedroom;
the memory of needing small places to dream;
my daughter's eyes—expressionless, watching.

2. homecoming

I think of the houses I lived in
as a child—how they seem
to get smaller every time I drive past them,
the little doorway puckering shut,
the yard like a handkerchief, pilled with grey weeds,
the windows no bigger than pin-pricks.

Driving past them, I imagine that if
I got out of the car, made my way
down the cracked concrete sidewalk
past the doddering medusas
of the plums my parents planted
forty years back, I'd be greeted
by my mother, now no bigger
than a Beatrix Potter fieldmouse
chittering brittle vowels at me
as I wobble up the concrete steps,
this monster who was once her kid,
and drone out my dull adult small-talk.

Invited inside, I'd find my dad
relaxing in a match-box chair, looking much
as he always did, though his head
is a clothes-peg, and his pipe-cleaner arms
are holding up a scrap of cloth
on which are scribbled the minuscule glyphs
of some embryonic language.

Later, after plates of dust
and seeds from the pitiful garden,
I'd stagger back out of the past to my car,
my mind a bruised rain-cloud, my veins
knotted roads, and drive away frantically,
anywhere, everywhere, into the hills
shame pouring over me, pervasive
as rain, all the route maps
curled up like scythed thistles.

3. the clientele

My daughter, who has just turned three,
observes me as I cut and fit, monitors my progress,
approves of the arrangement of rooms
or does not. When the walls have been cut
and the three floors are fitted
carefully into their rabbets and secured
with a long worm of carpenter's glue, she places
her eye to each window and inspects
the interior, her face an expressionless planet,
her mind drifting into each miniature room
thinking *nest and womb, enclosing cave,*
the idea of safety and shelter. Or conversely
imagining borders, herself in that house,
ensnared in the sad geometry
of husband, children, boring work,
her father's inane expectations—
seeing prison cell, ivory tower, cloister,
dungeon from which there can be no escape
except through a metamorphosis
so absolute her soul will shrink
to the size of match-stick doll's
painted-on heart. Or expand
almost infinitely out of her body
until her senses float like rings around Saturn
and her nerve-endings register nothing
but the blank hum of space, endless space.

4. the inhabitants

are anyone: Mom and Dad, Grandpappy,
Buddy and Sis, even little kids, pussycats
and doggies. Their lives are exactly
what your life would be, if your body
were constructed of wire and dowels
and you were dressed up in oddments
from Frieda's Fabric Barn. Building people
isn't challenging, as everyone knows. Babies
can be made just by cutting the heads
off discarded wooden clothes-pegs. Their extremities
are pipe-cleaners, supple yet stiff.

It suits them, inevitably, to pretend we don't exist,
to confuse us with landforms, atmospheric events,
the predictable workings of physics.
They observe us from their little windows,
our faces vast as nebulae, our fingertips
whorled stars and planets, saying
*mountain, cloud, stand of trees, setting
sun. UFO. Comet.* Then, jostling down
the toothpick sash and closing
the gingham swatch curtains,
they sit at their miniature desks and reduce us
to geometric figures, equations. We are moving
away from each other at nearly
the velocity of light, they have decided.

This, of course, is undeniable: my daughter,
for example, has already begun to lose interest
in this little world her father is building
for her; her bored gaze anticipates
the obsolescence of this archetypal household:
Already, in her mind, it's been consigned to dead space,
wombed in a childhood too quickly cast off,
the tiny rooms blurred into archives of dust,
the baffled dolls sleeping like pharaohs.

5. the staircase

goes nowhere, but fold it up anyway,
the step and the rise a bare half-inch each,
and affix it securely to the livingroom wall
with a dab of glued smeared on a toothpick.

Tonight, in your dreams, the glue will have set,
and the runner, a skinny swatch of jazzy mauve velvet
cut from the hem of your wife's cast-off blouse,
will stream down toward you, dense as light from the moon.

A child again, you will get up and sleepwalk
in your rumpled pajamas through the rooms of the house,
up the stairs to that blank space, behind which
your parents' voices, indecipherable
as the shrieking of demented birds,
mutter and rant at each other
through the peeling mac-tac paper on the plywood.

This staircase has always existed
at the end of the tunnel you entered in sleep;
the blank wall, as well, has always been there.
You have sat on the top step forever like that,
a child with a middle-aged man's weathered face,
miniature, forlorn, hardly listening.

6. *decorating*

Isabel chooses her colours: exterior walls
the bland blue of a comic-book sky, the rooms
gold as honeycombs, flashbulbs of light,
the hallways red as vivisected arteries. I daub
with a one-inch brush, transforming the wood
from nature into something more perfect—
materials unheard of except in cartoons,
animate window-frames, edible bricks,
doorways that speak with weird accents.

7. *moving day*

Completed, the new dollhouse squats on a desk.
When the paint has dried, my daughter gets busy.
Her blue-grey eyes thoughtful, she examines the house,
then begins to place tables and beds in the rooms,
her fingers, still chubby with baby-fat but marvelously deft,
positioning appliances and wooden-spool tables,
tugging the drapes back and forth on their threads,
arranging the postage-stamp paintings.

The dolls seem to huddle at the front of the house,
avoiding the open rear side of the building.
They busy themselves with their chores or TV,
a family of agoraphobics, each one coping bravely
with the terror of plummeting out into space,
of losing themselves in the uncertain precincts
that lie beyond the green felt yard, the fragile toothpick fences.

I understand their apprehension perfectly; it's a concern
that is common to both humans and dolls,
the fear of being wrenched out of context,
I recognize it, for example, in my daughter—
the confusion I see in her eyes when her mother
and I raise our voices in anger, her reluctance to give up
first the breast, then the soother she uses
to mumble herself into comforting darkness,
her silence as she populates
this equivocal world that we've made.

There now, the last of the dolls is positioned
near the foot of her bed in a room gold as money.
My little girl smiles up at me, her eyes
grey as hoarfrost. What she sees,
of course, is nothing much:
her father's face, a stenciled moon;
a universe of tinfoil stars;
the ordinary furniture of heaven.

There are some nights when I watch my son
asleep beneath his home-stitched quilt,

so beautiful and still I have to touch
his cheek to reassure myself
he's real, and whole, and breathing,

and find myself thinking of another man's child
who must have been about the age
my boy is now
on the last day his own father knew him.

I imagine him, this stolen boy,
as I know that he cannot be—
alive and whole, but lost within
the forest of his weightless dreams:

I wish that I could speak to him,
try to offer him some solace;

whisper what anyone's father would,
if only to the hollow place
in the grass at the edge of the clearing

where he lay before he turned to wind
under blankets of torn kites and hawks' wings.

Listen, I would say to him,
there is nothing left to wait for:

the deer are still invisible;
there are several moons to choose from;

you can walk across this field toward your life.

PART THREE

NOAH DREAMS

—for Mike

Your friends say the last thing
you did before you died
was take your paintings
and sculptures to the city dump
in the bed of your pickup and burn them.

This could be pure bullshit, but I guess it should do
as mythology, anyway: I think of you sometimes,
going off without your artist's mask
of bitter twigs and kestrel's bones, naked
as anyone gets in this life, stripped

like some Faust of your memories and books,
left finally with nothing
but the haywire nerves that flashed and failed,
the intractable weight of the body.

If I remember you now, it's as you were in the story
you told me twenty years ago—halfway
to the Charlottes in a wooden-hulled tug
towing a jet boat, a houseboat, a listing barge;
pulled down by whatever you needed

to make a life or end a life. And then
for Christ's sake running into
the dead calm and a shoal of fog
so thick you couldn't have found your ass
with both hands and a compass. You entered it
against your will, cognizant of the tonnage,
the numb weight you had strung astern,

and as lost as you were, I imagine
you feeling as you threaded north,
balanced on the thermalcline,
the way Coyote must have felt
in the moment that followed Creation
when he saw that whatever the world was, was his
and that anything he could ever build
from that wrack of possibilities
vague as a wall of west coast fog
would cast an indelible shadow.

You'll forgive me, I guess, if I leave you like that
23 years old or whatever,
pigheaded as the rest of us,
the blank world ahead of you, all the cardinal points
of the compass lost,
except of course the fluent eye
shaping art from the everyday flotsam.

I picture you now as you might have been then,
crazy hippie kid, hunched in the wheelhouse
peering out into the fog's blank word,
obscured by your own blurred reflection,
and hearing, above the slap of waves,
a rustle of wings from other lives—

your fair share of hope
and despair arcing back,

the black bird and the white bird.

PIT HORSES

—for my grandfather, dying

On the first day of the colliers' strike
he rises at dawn from the pit-head,
above ground on a working day
for the first time he can think of
since he turned 13, emerges
at last from the hole
of his birth into light, his eyes
the grey of thunderheads, his cheekbones
blacked with coal dust. His hands,
involved in leather reins,
tug gently at the bridles
of the sightless white draught-horses
used to draw coal
over sloping tracks, deep in the mine shaft.

As he walks, his voice repeats their names,
Gwawr, Brenhines, Milwr, Cymreig
sounding each like the stroke
of a pick against stone. He hammers
their names into daylight. The fields
at the pit head are bruised with black slag,
through which, like small miracles
soft grass blades nudge up. The air
is the grey-white of nights without sleep.

My grandfather tugs at the bridles
and leads the blind white horses out
of earth, unbinds their fetlocks
from weight of chains and harness straps
the necessity of hauling
gravity from the planet's core

black mineral out of bedrock. Blind, the horses
twitch in wind
that has never blown on earth before
their eyelids stabbed by light, the bells
of their vast hooves
cupped like ears to the ground,
their chancred haunches shifting. He walks
between them through the blasted field
of light, toward this moment,

this bed on which he lies
tonight, his hair
blanched white as winter straw,
his ear against the brittle sheet
still listening for
the thunder of
blind hooves along the mine shaft.

NEAR THE GRAVE OF AMELIA EARHART

the researchers from America,
having hacked their way
through canes as sharp
as razors, found the coffin
of a native child, dead a couple of years—

a box, the size of an orange crate,
made of green wood, which had sprouted
a web of saplings
like the veins around a heart,
which, split with the blade
of a labourer's machete, revealed
a nest of bones so frail they might
as well have belonged to some bird
as a child. For a moment, the men
were deceived by the fineness
of the bones into thinking
that the tibia and clavicle, the brown
spinal knuckles of the child
contained in the green
living womb of that box
were the wrist-bones and fingers

of Amelia. Each man, at that moment,
let his mind fill with wings, remembered
how the long-vanished girl
had come shuddering up
through the hard doubt of men
and the dubious machines,
the dark scars of airstrips
healed over with bush,

the irrational language
of weather. Each thought
of her slim hips and pale
boyish face, her legs
in stiff trousers, her narrow
men's shoes, and believed
that she still circled somewhere
in the fog of lost years, the lights
of her old haywire Lockheed like stars
at mid-day, her voice on the wireless
pure silence. The Islanders hired
to cut cane and clear brush
rocked back on their heels,
let the blades of their machetes
reflect the full sun
until each held an arc
of white fire in his fist
and the foreigners winced
in bald sunlight. The waves

arcing up on the beach
were clear fire, and the skull
of the Lockheed lay on coral, fathoms down
where the shelf of the reef
had sheared off in high winds
and the wound of Amelia's descent
through the trees gone crumbling down
with the steel bones of her airplane
into water. Days later
someone found her shoe, a plain
brown oxford, laced, size nine,
the rubber Catspaw heel intact
as if she'd set one hesitant foot
on earth before she vanished.

LEARNING TO SWIM AT FORTY

Letting go, diving straight for the heart
of the lake isn't easy—The body,
for one thing, resists it,

discovers reserves of buoyancy,
bobs stubbornly back to the surface,
being lighter than any element

but the light itself, which has deepened
perceptibly now at the edge of things,
a stain moving out of the mountain

and over the mirroring skin of the lake
into which she seems, floating
to have fallen from the sky.

Subtle waves shimmer back
from her wake as she swims—the decade
between us, its meaningless sheen,

comes rippling back through the dark
to my heart. I am empty
of hope now; the soul does not float,

though the body, inexplicably,
maintains an equilibrium
between this fading evening sky

and the deep, inarticulate colours
of lakebottom debris, dead branches,
past lives. Spuming out lakewater, probably

rancid with duck shit, I frog-kick
and flail in my haphazard breast stroke,
making for the core of things—

that one remaining brilliant patch
of water where my young wife turns
to fire, her blonde hair burning.

NELLY, DREAMING

1.

Listen: Not once in all the years
she and I have shared this bed
have I allowed myself
to fall asleep, not even
for a moment: each night
I lie awake and watch
her walking backwards, falling
gradually into her infancy, her body
getting smaller and smaller
like one of those Ukranian dolls
that contains its own miniature image.

Men do this—we are watchers,
we consider it our duty
to remain awake, recording
in our simple hearts
the thoughts of our sleeping beloved,
noting how she sighs and turns,
adrift among submarine longings;

how her shadow leaks back
into the hulls of her discarded slippers,
capsized on the throw-rug, life-boats washed up
from the wreck of some liner
torpedoed on its maiden voyage
toward the distant, desert shores
of motherhood and marriage;

how her breath turns to frost
on the limbs of bleak alders
as she flees across the tundra
pursued by cartoon wolves and centaurs on crutches
toward the bulbous onion domes
of her childhood, that mythical kingdom.

Such vigilance is the heavy price
of loving a beautiful woman,
though from whom or what I'm supposed to be
protecting her is mysterious—perhaps
I am only rehearsing, preparing
myself for the life to come,
the inevitable hour of departure,
prelude of torch songs and Pathé News battles,
when I'll stand on the platform
under grimed squares of starlight
in Grand Central Station
and witness her waving
a handkerchief perfumed
with regrets and excuses
as she offers one long, languid
wave from the express train
that conveys her into narrative,
the opera her expectant heart
is writing in her dreams.

2.

Almost every night she talks in her sleep
not conversing with me, but uttering
dialogue from some obscure *film noir*
in which her sleeping mind has a bit part—
not the ingenue but someone else
Blonde Girl in Restaurant,
Distraught Woman #3,
Or, more frequently, Second Victim.

Night after night, she is crying
out from the wings of a sound stage
dismantled forty years ago, screaming
*Faster! Speed up! They're gaining
on us!* I wake up, bolt upright
in bed, my heart thumping,
and lie there beside her,
staring wildly into simple dark
like a drunk waking up in a theatre
to discover that the feature is over,
the projectionist and ushers gone,
the house lights up, the janitor
muttering as he scrapes his broom
through the refuse of virtual romances.

My wife, meanwhile, has cuddled up
and drifted off to sleep again, her brow smooth,
her lips pursed, her body a contour map
of some hilly republic where everyone lives
in transmontaine meadows as soft as duvets.

As for me, I can't get a moment's rest—
I keep expecting her to call me
"Lefty" or "Fingers"; I imagine her
struggling, trapped in a burning
scenario, her pumps clacking helplessly
around the chalk outlines
of abandoned hopes, forsaken
lovers, adolescent crushes.

"What's your racket, Mister?" she'll ask suddenly,
addressing not me but the pocket
of nothingness, warmed by her breath,
between her lips and a fold of the percale.

I admit it's a troubling question. What place
does a mere husband have in the dark
of his sleeping wife's bijou subconscious?
Neither Sam Spade nor Marlowe, he mopes
around the sound stage, a character-actor written out
of every scene but the last one
in which he's the jaded reporter
too late to do anything but chain-smoke and scribble
the same clichéd cut-line as always:

Slumbering starlet sees slayings
in sleep. Sonambulant husband suspected.

CONSPICUOUS CONSUMPTION

In my dream I was holding an animal, she says.
And then it turned into a baby. She is possibly
the clerk in this store—who can tell? She is talking
to the customers as if they were her closest friends.
They nod, they smile, they have dreams of their own
to explain to passers-by; while they speak,
the girl collapses on a sofa, crosses her legs
beneath her green velvet gown, stifles a yawn,
and ignores them. Here everything
is something else—this store is someone's
livingroom, commerce is method acting,
psychiatry is jazz, this sales-clerk is a limp
Modigliani. Oh look, I tell my little son,
this cushion is a star. I hold it up, yellow
as a marigold, tasseled as an ear of corn,
many-legged as a starfish. Let's buy it! he urges.
He mounts a wrought-iron rocking horse
and charges toward the future. What's your policy
on refunds? I enquire of the languid salesclerk.
You're a man, she says accusingly,
You wouldn't understand. She's right,
of course—I comprehend so little now.
My therapies have left me bald;
I'm thinking of having a transplant.
I've been dreaming of horses again, the girl goes on.
They charged across the fields to me, those phallic necks
lunging obscenely. It was raining
punctuation marks. My period
was ten years late. My lover's eyes were commas.
Life's like that, though, isn't it, I have to admit:
Nothing's ever what it seems to be—
Question marks, horses, ellipses, pale stars.
I proffer my Master Card, so many years expired.
She clings to it, breathless, exalted.

PART FOUR

All through second period, the boy
who sits behind me has been eating
yellow roses. When the teacher's eyes
are on her book, I turn in my desk and watch him.
He carefully peels each petal from the rose
he's holding, taking his own sweet time,
then ribbons it up with his smoker's teeth
and swallows. Mrs Parkins, for her part, ignores him.

What does she care? He's failed two grades already.
All year he has slouched at the back of the class,
the collar of his leathers up, preening
his duck-ass with a pink rat-tailed comb.
Two months from now, he'll black my eye
by accident, the two of us boxing
for the fear of it, slipping on tiles in the boys' room.
Next summer, he'll open his madras shirt
one day while we're watching the girls at the lake
and show me his breasts. *You'd better not
call me a queer!* he'll say, his green eyes admitting
one pure flash of terror, a millisecond long—
calm waters ablaze with blank lightning.

The teacher drones through Tennyson,
stalking the aisles with a slow, limping step.
All around her, teenagers slump in their desks,
bodies limp, drowning eyes lidded.
When she gets to the line about
the knight with a chink in his armor, the tallest girl
in Grade Eight laughs—one tight, shrill bark—
then apologizes to her closest friend,
the daughter of our local Chinese grocer.

Later on, when the heroine
expires out of love, Alice Chalmers, who lives
in a house-trailer next to the Esso with her dad,
a bricklayer too sickened with whiskey to work,
flashes her pale eyes and bruised, bitter mouth
from the nest of her red hair, straight at me.
For the rest of the period, I stare at her back
and wonder if she knows I'd like
to bury my teeth in the flesh of her neck—
mottled white, starred with red freckles—
lick the skin between her sweaty breasts,
coax open her damp thighs and shag her.

On and on, Mrs Parkins plods through her poems,
doling out Art with a soup-kitchen spoon,
her nasal voice ladling rhyme after rhyme,
half-hectoring, half-weepy. The boy
who sits behind me flicks
the stem of his denuded flower
into Wanda Klossky's cashmere lap.
She sneers, reveals her rose-pink tongue.

The iambs of the risen word
clatter like crows through the neon.

VASECTOMY

1.

Just relax, the Doc tells me.
All right: I stretch out
on the ass-freezing gurney, shut my eyes and drift back
to a chill October sunrise, the year I was twelve.
The doctor's needle mines my crotch. I wait
for the numbness, trudge stunned through deep bush.
My old man's gone hunting. I'm tagging along
with a cousin and one of my uncles,
the men hunched and watchful, bolt-action
Lee Enfields in the crooks of their arms,
Cousin Jimmy and me packing torches.
It's six in the morning and just getting light;
we've been humping our asses since daybreak,
tramping uphill through sodden salal
and the acrid smell of burning. There's nothing
to hunt but the rumour of blood, not even
black berries of spoor in the muck
churned up by our well-dubbined
Kodiacs—just nothing. We crest a bare volcanic ridge
and crouch with our backs to the dawn, peering down
through a puzzle of swamp-cedar branches.

Who in hell'd live out here? Uncle Don
says, and spits. Some people'd pitch a tent
in a goshdarned latrine. The air
smells of punkwood and smouldering leaves.
Near the shack below, a scrawny man guts corpses
and hangs them on hooks—two bucks,
by the look of it, the other a doe. Their innards
hoard flies by the lean-to. *Pit-lampers,*
Jimmy whispers. He's wrong, though: a girl
about my age comes out of the shack. On some instinct,
she looks up and searches the bush
until the prick of her spooked gaze locates us.

2.

Let me know if there's any discomfort,
the doctor says. *It affects some men differently*
than others. For the next three days, my scrotum
bleeds purple and ignorant black, plumps up
with my blood like a game bird
that's riddled with buckshot and strung up to age.
You can live off the land if you have to:
Venison, pine mushrooms, animal flesh,
the seep of jaundiced light between
these screw-pine boughs and scrub-oak.

My old man squints and spits a gob
of Skoal between his hunting boots.
Every living thing on earth, he observes,
exists to be shot down and gutted.
The afternoon swings there, hung up
on a hook. *There's always an element*
of risk, the Doc says. *But I'm 99% certain*
you're sterile. The examination
cut off, he smiles and stalks out. I dress myself
cautiously, favouring my crotch,
and amble outside into insolent light.
In a farm-truck outside the clinic, a girl
glances up from her swaddled child,
mumbling one breast; the young mother
half-stripped and sinuous-necked as a doe
in the mulch of deep rainforest, spooked by a step.
Cousin Jimmy and I slide
down the sidehill, angling our boots
into shit-yellow clay, clutching saplings
to steady our balance. When we get
to the clearing, the girl holds her ground
by her dad's side and watches us,
awkward in alder-shade, huffing like bucks.
I wince from her gravid eyes, pit-lamped.

CLEAN

Twenty years along
our separate paths, I finally run into her,
shuffling through a shopping mall,
brass-blonde hair and battered boots,
trailing her plastic shopping bags
and staring through the aimless crowds
of shoppers as if she were seeing
not neon lights and lino floors, but somewhere
hoarded from a sad child's dream
the far rocks of a headlong stream,
sunlit, unreachably distant—
Jeanne Duval in exile at
the gates of the Country Club WalMart.

You got any kids? she asks,
and right then, no doubt about it, there's something
needful in her grey-blue eyes, as if she thirsts
to feel the mundane tides
that tug me back to work and home,
even second-hand, from a distance.

I tell her about my boy and girl, trying not
to sound too full of them. She fusses with her Ultra-lash,
as though a mote of bitter light has lodged
in the angle of one hard blue eye,
and reveals a jailhouse butterfly
indelible as an aurochs
just above the frayed black denim cuff
in the skin of her delicate wrist.

Not me, she says, you know how it is.
All those years of cranking scag and all
pretty much fucked up my innards. That wasn't
what I wanted then—me and Danny, well,
you knew him. I guess I didn't understand
what it was he had a jones for, though.

When the paramedics closed his eyes,
he looked so fucking smug. I've been clean,
you know, for eighteen months.
There's a gang of us get together now
in the coffee bar at Smitty's. They're giving me
a cake tonight, it's a kind of celebration.

I smile, not knowing what to say.
Our eyes meet, then we glance away,
afraid to be seen to be searching
for the palimpsest of wasted youth
eroded to a fossil trace,
the child's hurt flinch in the adult's face.
We watch the plodding shoppers.

"I better head along," she sighs.
I smile again and watch her go,
putting one foot in front of the other
along the glaring market aisle,
stepping carefully, as if she walked on stones,
the near shore bleak and masked
with cloud, the distance barely brighter.

FUNERAL RITES

Our cat keeps killing rabbits. All spring
she's been leaving their parts on the porch,
rodent skulls neatly bisected,
what's left of the truncated cortex still dreaming
of the sweetness of swollen roots
and tender green buds; fuzzy
good-luck charms in Rorschach-blot blood;
bunny-tails slick with saliva. It's my job, inevitably,
to inter the dead. I do this reluctantly, scraping up
matted fur, disjointed limbs, organ meat
gleaming like ripe, ruptured berries
from the driveway and sidewalks, then swilling
blood from the concrete with the spray of a hose.

Less frequently, when the cat is at sport
or content with her canned food, I have to lift
a whole tiny corpse on the lip of a shovel,
observing the glazed eye,
the scraggly brown smoker's teeth, rusty as nails,
the long, fluted ears with their haloes of fuzz
ruffling like Biblical wheat in the wind
that blows across the farmer's fields
adjacent to our suburb,
flushing up swallows to the bruised evening sky.

Once or twice, I've had to use the blade
of the shovel to finish off the work
the idiotic cat began. Taking aim
on the soft, furred throat, I heave
the primitive implement over my head,
hesitate just long enough to focus
my mind on its petty excuses, then

blinking to banish the shiver of metaphor
that threatens to wedge in my spine
like a surgeon's hollow skewer, connecting
the spavined rabbit's wounded twitch
to my own body's quiverings, flinching
from harm, bring the blade down
like Abraham killing his son,
for a god like a housecat, its blank tinfoil eyes
reflecting not necessity, hunger, and fear,
but the whim of the senses to hunt, hurt, and kill.
The cat rolls and suns itself, watching.

CAYMAN BRACK
(My grandfather at ninety)

The storm last night was less severe
than that of the night before, but still
these rains cause inconvenience
dampening the coarse brown sand that surrounds
my dilapidated life, this dwelling.

Wet brown sand insinuates itself
into every crevice, returning
unwanted each day to the vanishing paths. Sisyphus, armed
with my wife's straw broom, I endlessly sweep
at the bothersome grit. Wet sand adheres
to my steps as I walk, the trace
of my days a palimpsest
of the trivial concerns that distract me.

The Cayman locals speak of storms. I imagine,
superstitiously, that the absence
of morning dew portends
the coming of a hurricane. The centre
of the storm is moving north; it lies
some miles from Savannah-la-Mar,
swirling the seas in a tight Celtic knot—
the voice of God speaking in ikons. You write
that Yseult, my sister, died: "very sad"
you remark, but remember
that I am that Platonic who sees
the immutable mould
in the shifting forms, the motionless eye

of the hurricane. Have I said
that my passport expires this October? I desire
more than anything else to escape
from this place: the planks
of the sunporch have warped
from the crossbeams; the old pump that drizzles

a gritty stream of water drawn
from the well beyond the road was hit
two nights ago by a fireball. For hours
the lightning came and went, neither forked tongues
nor zigzags, but shimmering balls
that hammered like fists at the shingles and walls,
grounding themselves on the downpipes. I wish
for storms to smash this house,
blast the sagging roof and rickety porch,
collapse the leaning chimney,

let my sullen wife and me go forth
naked through the fallen world, the rent veil
of outward appearance. Heavy rains before morning
caused an overflow of filth
from the septic tank twenty feet east
of this ruin. The mosquitos, at least,
have gone from the ponds, though the lice
of Heraclitus still plague me.

All night I read the Vedic hymns
of worship to Agni, Indra, Varuna.
Most recently, I have ascertained
that the greatest of cleansers
are Thunderbolt, Rainstorm,
Rotation of Earth, the various sons
of the demi-god Rudra the Roarer. I hear
within these leaking walls
no voice, but a wordless
hiss of wind. Listen...

More and more I believe
that of all the foods, fruits alone
are beneficial. Papaya is the strongest fruit,
apple the most natural, bananas no use

for anything, though the northerners
seem to prize them. These damnfool Caymanians,
existing on turtle meat, know nothing
of the proper cultivation of trees. They cover
the earth with hard brown sand, make up lies
about hurricanes and thunder. The ability
to conjure up falsehoods is required
by the sons of whores who practice
religion. Your great-grandfather often said:
"Christians, those liars!"
and from this the rumour spread that he
was a man who believed
in nothing—in fact
his beliefs were as multiform
as the petals of an antique rose.

I see my father's English roses
tangled on the gate; my memory burns
the image clear, the pale light
wanes and flickers. A wind rakes up
the cloudless air. Oh, yes

I would welcome a hurricane.

THERMODYNAMICS

I sit beside the angled bed, redundant
as the stiff bouquet of daffodils, browned
to the colour of tea-leaves, the blank
eye of the TV screen, the fields of neutered sunlight
just beyond these mud-grey walls.

Embarrassed, at a loss for words
as always when confronted with essentials
such as dying, I content myself
with waiting out her silences and nodding
encouragement when the eyelids twitch
and the hollow crow of her windpipe takes
the shapes of need and thought.

In the narrowing windows of breath
between seizures, she discourses on the flavour
of mangoes: how she'd pick them fresh
in Martinique, oval fruit soft as a breast
in her fingers, the slack flesh concealing a sweetness
so perfect her lips, drained to pallid magenta
from failing circulation, pucker at it thought of it
as she savours the ghost of sensation. Her teeth

after eighty years, are blunt
and worn as adzes. At twenty, though, she'd swim ahead
of the oyster-boat, holding a bow-line
in clenched jaws and towing
her husband past the coral reef,
the slack tide, the crumbling sea-wall,
glancing back across the swell of light
to glimpse him sitting upright—
his frock coat, his patriarchal whiskers—
great Moses on the fragrant flood
of memory, drifting out. *Her body
is shutting down,* the night nurse informs me.

I imagine the grid of her nerves going dark;
the hospital room folding into itself
one muddy beige petal at a time like origami
swans settling into the sweltering harbour;
the child in her muslin dress curled on the day-bed
in the Port-Au-Prince house, with its faint scent
of mangoes, sheltered at last
from the mad heat of being, the machinery
of pain and desire winding down,

all the energetic atoms of her body
whirling like flywheels and pulleys
backward toward the inertia,
the rest state that none of us comes from
but that each of us dreams in the end.

After she died, we began the task of cleaning up
my great-aunt's Gabriola house. The panabode, nestled
on a rock bluff facing Georgia Strait
turned out to be crammed to the rafters
with the detritus of eighty years, a lot of it translated
whole cloth from her life in Port-of-Spain.

Stacks of knick-knacks bulged the walls,
as if her cabin were a metaphor for aging:
the body's compass shrinking small, while still
the mind's profusions multiplied, and the solitary
heart dripped forth whole oceans. Before long
we'd turned up other metaphors: a family
of doleful orphan Teddy-bears, one holding
in ragged paws a threadbare edition
of Euclid; schools of dead electric clocks,
indentical white plastic ovals, each of them stuck
at exactly 8:20; and in the lingerie drawer a rapier
bright and venomous as a coral snake
among the intricacies of yellowed lace
and swooning folds of satin. My aunt herself
seemed mirrored in her myriad forms

like a Grecian temple-goddess: innocent, mad
lover, hearth-mother, saint. I encountered her
at six years old, under alien trees in a tropical orchard,
her eyes bright as garnets in sepia light;
smiling from early Kodachromes, jovial,
out-of-register, the world behind her changing
like a carnival backdrop, and lounging
in loose slacks, arrogant as Dietrich,
her breasts bare, her hand at the throttle
of a fifth of Baccardi's, in the arms
of some muscular yachtsman—the snapshots

both a record of fact and a symbol
for the headlong, self-shattering plummet
through the instants of life that transforms us
from a flame to a shower of sparks.

The last thing I packed was a bookcase, marooned
in the sewing room, wedged between beds,
inaccessible without shifting boxes
stuffed with brass surveyor's instruments,
far too heavy for a woman in her eighties to lift.
The shelves held a matched set of volumes—
the *Encyclopedia Brittanica*, v. 1
to 26, bound in dull amber leather,
the spines furred with dust. Curious, I pulled
Volume One from the shelf, pried it open
against the stiffness of decades: inside,
there was nothing but a network of holes, sinuous
cavities where bookworms, long vanished
themselves into dust, had reduced
those crisp linen pages to a web of grey lace.

All twenty-five other books were also
destroyed. I thought of the slow disappearing
of memory—how our fads and illuminations,
so painfully accrued through a lifetime of perceiving
like the atoms of silica in coral reefs, the cells
of some vast human body, decay
into spiral voids, labyrinths of open mouths
each gonging its quanta of nothingness
to echo through the dessicated honeycombs
that wormhole from unborn to gone.

OZONE

When the June rains come I watch the air
as the sky above the valley
goes bleak beneath a gourd of cloud,
takes on that flare of stellar green
that speaks of summer lightning.

I turn out the house-lights,
throw open every window,
slip off my shoes and make my rounds
through each of the rooms in the house I built,
barefoot, in no hurry,

at ease in the intimate blueprint
of whatever my heart
has made holy, understanding
the textures of maple lathe, ceramic and stone,
the worn fibre mat in the hallway.

When the first stab of light
tugs the rain taut as skin
on a drumhead, I am already watching.
Through the bedroom door I see my wife,
asleep on the peacock spread,

her feet smooth as shells,
our daughter curled into her belly,
the little girl's fingers unraveling knots
on her brief skein of memories, the woman
shuddering into some wind from her past.

I know them in a single pulse
of vision, then stand blinded;
their after-image ripples on my eyelids.
What I love is translucent, mere water,
like glimpsing the sun through a hawk's wing.

I could run through the fields now,
make jack-pine my bones,
curl up beneath sword-fern, lie numbed as the shale,
in the shadows of widow-makers, scrub-oak.

Instead, I stand mute in the hallway,
a man in the map of his habits,
alone for that blind, yearning instant
between the lightning's absolute
and the wholly mortal speed of sound,

the knife-blade scent of ozone.

WORK HABITS

My daughter brings me heron's bones,
knuckles of the arcing spine,
the shrill, piercing flutes of the wing-bones.
I place them on my writing-desk,
nodding *no* when she asks
if I can name them. When she leaves,
I think of metaphors: needle, syringe,
and cobbler's awl, a pin
for winkling *escargot*. My raw
heart retreats down its helix. In an hour,
the pen is weightless bone. I have sewn shut
my eyes. I am flying.